Seeing God's
GLORY

Jerry Yarnell

ISBN 979-8-89243-291-7 (paperback)
ISBN 979-8-89243-292-4 (digital)

Copyright © 2024 by Jerry Yarnell

All rights reserved. No part of this publication may be reproduced, distributed, or transmitted in any form or by any means, including photocopying, recording, or other electronic or mechanical methods without the prior written permission of the publisher. For permission requests, solicit the publisher via the address below.

Christian Faith Publishing
832 Park Avenue
Meadville, PA 16335
www.christianfaithpublishing.com

All Scripture is taken from the New American Standard Bible
Copyright 1997 by the Lockman Foundation.
Used by permission, www.lockman.org

Printed in the United States of America

This book is dedicated to the glory of the Lord and to my wife Pam. God brought her over fifty-two years ago in my life. She has sacrificed, enabled me, and ministered with me for the glory of God. I thank God for her. May the Lord God truly receive my thanks.

CONTENTS

Introduction..vii

Chapter 1: God's Glory...1

Chapter 2: Man's Eye Problem 10

Chapter 3: Soul Blinders 14

Chapter 4: Soul Binders II..19

Chapter 5: Soul Blinders III 22

Chapter 6: God's Prescription for Our Eyes.................28

Chapter 7: God's Prescription for Our Eyes II 35

Chapter 8: God's Prescription for Our Eyes III............41

Chapter 9: Seeing God's Glory 49

INTRODUCTION

"Mine eyes have seen the Glory of the coming of the Lord" is the familiar first line of the Battle Hymn of the Republic. It was written by Julia Ward Howe in 1861. Howe, being an Abolitionist, wrote this song, and it became a marching song for the Union Army in our Civil War. In verse two, she wrote," I have seen Him in the watchfires." Then, in verse four, she wrote, "In the beauty of the lilies Christ was born across the sea with a Glory in His being that transfigures you and me."

More than just a familiar nationalistic song, this hymn talks of SEEING GOD'S GLORY and how this Glory can be a powerful force in our lives. It raises an important question. Do you see the Lord's glory in your life? Do you want to see His Glory at work all around you?

My hope and prayer, my feeble effort here of writing, may help see better His Glory. Jesus talks of the BLESSING of seeing this Glory in Matthew 13:13 when He said.

> Therefore I speak to them in parables because while seeing they do not see and while hearing they do not hear, nor do they understand.

Jesus wasn't talking about Gentile unbelievers but about believing Jews of His time. They somehow didn't grasp the workings of God, for their lack of sight hindered them. In the following verse,

He cites the prophet Isaiah, who told of the reason for this condition. He said,

> In their case the prophecy of Isaiah is being fulfilled, which says, "You will keep on hearing, but will not understand, You will keep on seeing, but will not perceive: for the heart of This people has become dull. With their ears they scarcely hear, and they have closed Their eyes." (Matthew 13:14)

Quite an indictment, isn't it? It was true then, and the same could be said of many believers today. It is obvious that Jesus wants us to see and understand the Glory of God in this world and to understand His Word and the will God has for each of us. Paul, an avid Jewish believer, needed to see God's glory. It began with his conversion. But that was only the beginning of Paul. We need to see more clearly the glory of God so that we may be transfigured and changed. As with Paul, it isn't a one-time event.

> But we all with unveiled face beholding as in a mirror the glory of the Lord are being transformed into the same image from glory to glory just as from the Lord the Spirit. (2 Corinthians 3:18)

Seeing the glory of the Lord works to transform us—to change us into the people we were intended to be. As we see more clearly God's glory, we are being changed. As you seek to see more clearly the glory and works of the Lord, it will enable you and me to sing even louder that phrase from "Amazing Grace" and from John 9:25, "I was blind now I see!"

CHAPTER 1

God's Glory

No fewer than twenty-five Hebrew words are used for our word glory. They refer to the importance, weight, consideration, or work of God in his creation.

Some do refer to a person's riches or reputation, as in Psalm 49:16,

> Do not be afraid when a man becomes rich when the glory of his house is increased.

Likewise in Job's discourse in Job 29, we see it again applied to one's being or one's situation.

> My glory is ever new with me and my bow is renewed in my hand.

The term glory is also used to describe Israel's blessing by God in assuring them of His provision for victory.

> The Glory of Israel will enter Adullam (an enemy's land). (Micah 1:15)

These cases, it seems that the glory of God had blessed or made someone or something special. They, therefore, reflected the glory God had bestowed on them. Yet, for the most part, the term glory is used as a description of the work, presence, and power of God. The glory of God is the awesome presence of God, as seen by his work among his people and the world's people.

There were many times and ways God revealed his glory to his people in the Scriptures. He did this so that they could see Him working for them, and so they would seek a deeper relationship with Him. We can't list them all, but it is obvious that he reached out to his people so that they might know Him.

God's Glory Revealed in the Old Testament

The glory of God is revealed to us in His creation.

> The heavens are telling the glory of God. (Psalm 19:1)

St. Paul echoes this reality evident from the beginning of time when he wrote,

> That which is known about God is evident within them for God made it evident to them. For since the creation of the world His invisible attributes, his eternal power and divine nature has been clearly seen, being understood through what has been made. (Romans 1:19–20)

Just looking at the creation show should enable us to see and recognize God's mighty hand and glory. Yet so often, we may see beauty, but we fail to recognize the God of glory in the world we live in. It is obvious that the Lord's intent is that we see his glory and presence in His work; His real desire is to be in all relationships with us. God's desire goes beyond just seeing Him in His creation. Moses experienced the Lord in his encounter with the fire of the burning

SEEING GOD'S GLORY

bush that was not consumed by the fire. A voice spoke to him from the fire and bush and called to him from the midst and said,

> Moses, Moses! And he said, "Here I am." And then He said, "Do not come near here; remove your sandals from your feet for the place in which you are standing is holy ground." (Exodus 3:4–5)

Like the Hebrews, we are called to see God's glory and his provision for us. During their journey through the wilderness, the Hebrews began to grumble against Moses and Aaron. It seems they forgot God's working in the plagues and in the Red Sea to deliver them. So God gave them manna and meat so that they may know his presence with them.

> So Moses and Aaron said to all the sons of Israel. At evening you will know that the Lord has brought you out of the land of Egypt and in the morning, you will see the glory of the Lord. Exodus 16:6–7

We, too, are called to see His glory in His provision for us in our pasts and not to forget Him in our relationship with Him.

Later in Exodus, the people gathered at the base of Mount Sinai, and God told them that they would see His glory. As the people gathered, Moses went up to the mountain, and God again showed His presence and glory to Moses and the people.

> The glory of the Lord rested on Sinai in the cloud covered it for six days. (Exodus 24:16)

The glory of the Lord covered Mount Sinai with the cloud. And out of the cloud, the voice of the Lord spoke. There was to be no doubt that the Lord God was with them even in that wilderness. God revealed the glory in order that the people might know that He was with them and would lead them to the promised land. They would be led by a pillar of cloud during the day and a pillar of fire at night. This is done to assure them of His great love for them in a way they could see His glory reflected in the cloud and in the fire.

Although one would think they would be assured of his grace and presence, God went even further and had them build a tabernacle. This was to be a place of worship. And it was to be in the middle of the tribes, and when they were moving, it would go before them.

> Now, on the day the tabernacle was erected. The cloud covered the tabernacle, the tent of the testimony and any evening it was like the appearance of fire over the tabernacle until morning so was continuously; the cloud would cover it by day and the appearance of fire by night. (Number 9:15–16) (see also Exodus 40–34)

There was also a tent for meeting as a part of this worship complex. Although the people could not enter it, Moses and Aaron (who was called to be a priest) were allowed to enter this tent. The presence of God was made known to all through Moses and Aaron.

> Moses and Aaron went into the tent of meeting. When they came out and bless the people the glory of the Lord appeared to all the people. (Leviticus 9:23)

People of that time had many opportunities to see God's glory, but sadly, they tended to forget when they approached the land God was going to give them. They stopped, sending spies to check it out. All but two came back saying not to enter the land because the land "Devours its inhabitants and all the people whom we saw in it are men of great size" (Numbers 13:32).

Just a lack of faith angered the Lord, and Moses prayed that the Lord would forgive them and turn away his anger for their lack of trust. He gave them that the lack of trust would mean forty years of

SEEING GOD'S GLORY

wandering in the wilderness. God reveals His plan for the people that was thwarted by their lack of trust.

> So the Lord said, "I have pardoned them according to your word; but indeed as I live, all the earth will be filled with the glory of the Lord. Surely all the men who see my glory and my signs which I performed in Egypt and in the wilderness yet have put me to the test 10 times and have not listen to my voice, shall by no means see the land which I swore to their father, nor shall any of those who spurn me see it." (Numbers 14:20–23)

Even today, there are consequences for seeing God's glory and failing to walk obediently with Him. Seeing His glory helps us in our living, knowing, and walking with Him. Seeing His glory is to be transfigured into people more like Him and how we were meant to be.

There are other instances where God displayed his glory, such as Numbers 16:42, Numbers 20:6, and 2 Chronicles 5:14. Another example of God's many displays of His glory, we turn to when Solomon dedicated the new temple. A glorious event took place at this dedication.

> When Solomon had finished praying, a fire came down from heaven and consumed the burnt offering and the sacrifices and the glory of the Lord filled the house. The priest cannot enter into the house of the Lord because the glory of the Lord filled the Lord's house. (2 Chronicles 7:1–2)

Fire and cloud were once again vehicles of the manifestation of God's presence, power, and glory. Remember Elijah at Mount Carmel in the contest with the priest of Baal? (1 Kings 18:22–39). Remember God's deliverance of Shadrach, Meshach, and Abednego?

In the midst of human trouble, God displayed His power and glory once again in fire (Daniel 3:13–26). There were many other times God revealed His glory in His deeds and his provision. God and his people could know Him and see His glory, but they couldn't live in a safe relationship with Him.

God's Glory Revealed in the New Testament

God displayed His glory for all of us to see, as cited before, the Word of God tells us,

> For the wrath of God is revealed from heaven against all ungodliness and unrighteousness of men who suppress the truth in unrighteousness, because that which is known about God is evident within them for God made it evident to them. For since the creation of the world his invisible attributes, his eternal power and divine nature had been clearly seen, being understood through what has been made, so that they are without excuse. (Romans 1:18–20)

It is obvious God desires all to see and enjoy His glory and presence prep. In the New Testament, God reveals his glory as He did in the Old Testament in a cloud at Christ's Transfiguration.

> While he was saying this cloud formed and began to overshadow them; and they were afraid as they entered the cloud. Then a voice came out of the cloud saying, "This is my Son, my chosen one; listen to him!" (Luke 9:34–35)

Matthew also wrote of this in his gospel chapter 17:5.

The Lord's glory was also manifested to the shepherds announcing the birth of the Savior.

SEEING GOD'S GLORY

> And an angel of the Lord suddenly stood before them and the glory of the Lord shone around them and they were terribly frightened. But the angel said to them, "Do not be afraid, for behold I bring you good news of great joy which will be for all people; for today in the city of David there has been born a Savior who is Christ the Lord." (Luke: 2:9–11)

The big change in the New Testament came with the ministry of Jesus. Now the glory of God was to be seen in the works and person of Jesus. He was called the light of men:

> In Him was life and the life was the light of men. (John 1:4)

At the Cana wedding, after turning the water into wine we read,

> This beginning of his signs Jesus did in Cana of Galilee and manifested His glory and his disciples believed in Him. (John 2:11)

Jesus was our incarnate God. He was God in the flesh. God's glory was to be seen in His works, signs, and wonders. At the Last Supper, after Judas had left to betray again, Jesus comforts His disciples after He tells them of His imminent death. He then tells them.

> I am the way the truth and the life no one comes to the Father but through me. If you had known me you have known my Father also. From now on you know him and have seen him. Philip said to him "Lord show us the Father and it is enough." Jesus said to him, "Have I been so long with you, and yet you have not come to know me Philip? He who has seen me has seen the Father." John 14:6–9

Jesus was the Father. His presence was the glory of God with us. The works, words, and miracles were the glory of the power of God and evidence of God's mighty works. Later, Jesus tells Philip and the other ten disciples,

> That I am the Father and the Father is in me otherwise believe because of the works themselves. (John 14:11)

The disciples were told that they had seen the glory of God and the signs and wonders and words of Jesus. While John the Baptist wasn't present, he sent some of his disciples asking Jesus if He was the Christ as he had believed.

> Now when is John, while in prison, heard of the works of Christ. He sent word by his disciples and said to Him, "Are you the expected one or shall we look for someone else?" Jesus answered and said to them, "Go report to John what you have heard and seen the blind receive sight and the lame walk, the lepers are cleansed and the deaf hear the dead are raised up and the poor have the Gospel preached to them." (Matthew 11:2–5)

In the words and works of Jesus to the people of that day, they were to see God's glory—and were able to see the glory of the Lord. Paul's letters are filled with praise for the glory of God in thanksgiving for his grace in Jesus the Lord and Savior! The disciple John, being in the Spirit, was given a vision of the second coming of the Lord Jesus. It is filled with the glory of God (Rev. 15:8, 21–14, and 21:23). All of this is recorded for us, so we live, see, and seek the Lord and His glory. We see the greatest act of God's love and glory on the cross. The Lord and Savior willingly gave up His life so that we might be forgiven and have eternal life in the presence of God.

SEEING GOD'S GLORY

God, give us eyes to see your glory in all that you have done. As we read your Word, open our eyes so that we may understand the great love you have for us. Help us to have eyes that see and ears that hear.

CHAPTER 2

Man's Eye Problem

At creation, God created us humans as the last and best of his creation. As the Scriptures tell us,

> What is man that you thought of him and the son of man that you care for him? Yet, you've made him a little lower than God and you crown him with glory and majesty. (Psalm 8:4–5)

What is the crown of his creation is that we were made in his image.

> Then God said, let us make man in our image according to our likeness. (Genesis 1:26)

What made us different from the animals? We were made in the Lord's image, and we were given something very special.

> Then the Lord God formed man of dust from the ground and breathed into his nostrils the breath of life and man became a living being. (Genesis 2:7)

SEEING GOD'S GLORY

God created us. He made us so that we could have fellowship with Him so we could enjoy Him. We were different than the animals because he made us with a living soul, so we could love him. He gave us three parts of our being so He can fulfill His desires for us to seek and want a relationship with Him. Paul recognized this when he wrote,

> Now may the God of peace Himself sanctify you entirely. May your spirit and soul and body be preserved complete, without blame at the coming of our Lord Jesus Christ. (1 Thessalonians 5:23)

We see a similar description of the distinction between our spirit and our soul.

> For the Word of God is living and active and sharper than any two-edged sword, piercing as far as the division of soul and spirit…. (Hebrews 4:12)

These two verses, as others do, show that the breath of God's creation made us body, soul, and spirit. Our body, with his five senses (sight, hearing, taste, smell, and feeling), helps us experience the world we live in. Our soul, made up of our will, intellect, and emotions, is what makes up who we are. All quarterly of this. Gives us the ability to know and relate to God.

We were meant to be spirit-driven beings, driven by our connection with God.

This was God's intended creation that we, like Adam and Eve, could walk with God in the cool of the evening in paradise. We need not go into great detail about the fall of man and the entrance of sin. Yet, it would help us understand our struggle by looking at the temptations of Satan carefully. We see the temptations were directed at the soul. First, he questioned our intellect (thinking) when he questioned Eve, saying, "You will not die." This was to get us to question our thinking process rather than to trust the word of God.

Then, the attack is at our will. Who wouldn't want to become a God, and we no longer would be one of God's creations? This appeared to be good, so in the attack of our emotions and that was complete. The fall of man made us "soulish-led creatures" as opposed to being led by the spirit. We began to live lives based on what we think, what we feel, and what we want.

Our spirit became what I like to call "deadened." We were no longer led by our spiritual connection to God, and we, like Adam and Eve, at times would hide from God.

> They heard the sound of the Lord God walking in the garden. In the cool of day, and the man and his wife hid themselves among the trees of the garden. (Genesis 3:8)

God, in John's gospel, says it this way, talking about Jesus as God's ever ardent desire to reach his creation.

> There was a true light which, coming into the world, enlightens every man. He was in the world, and the world was made through Him the world did not know him. (John 1:9–10)

And

> This is the light has come into the world all men loved darkness rather than the light for their deeds were evil. (John 3:19)

Soulish driven, we often seek things that our soul (will, intellect, and emotions) desires. When we begin to trust our souls and neglect the word and glory of God, we are led further away from His love and purpose for us. We then experience many pains and struggles

SEEING GOD'S GLORY

brought on by our failure to seek God in all situations and struggles. As the hymn, "What a Friend We Have in Jesus" says,

> Oh what peace we often forfeit, Oh what need-less pain we often bear. All because we do not carry everything to him in prayer.

Let us dig deeper into the sin that our soul brings us to when we fail to avail ourselves of the gift God has given us in our creation. That is the ability to know God as a spiritual being.

CHAPTER 3

Soul Blinders

Workhorses, as well as racehorses, often had a set of blinders over the side of their eyes. These blinders were to keep the horses from being distracted and to keep them focused on the task before them. In the opposite way, our soul gives us blinders that keep us focused on our intellect, will, and emotions. These blinders keep us from seeing God's glory, His works, and His signs that show us His presence and power. Thence, we fail to recognize His calling us to a love relationship with Him.

Intellect

We don't realize that our way of thinking is infected by sin. Yet our thinking without the Spirit and the Word is flawed. The Scripture calls us to rely on and trust God and not our own thinking.

> Trust in the Lord with all your heart. And do not lean on your own understanding. (Proverbs 3:5)

And

> There is a way which seems right to a man, but its end is the way of death. (Proverbs 14:12)

SEEING GOD'S GLORY

It is no wonder why the Lord, through Paul, tells us,

> And do not be conformed to but be transformed by the renewing of your mind so that you may prove what the will of God is, that which is good and acceptable and perfect. (Romans 12:2)

Again, He tells us to check out our thinking.

> We are destroying speculations and every lofty thing raised up against the knowledge of God, and we are taking every thought captive to the obedience of Christ. (2 Corinthians 10:5)

Failure to heed these warnings from our Lord, our thinking can be like those Isaiah talked about when he said,

> Woe to those who call evil good and good evil. (Isaiah 5:20)

It is so easy for us to think that something is good and fail to recognize that everything is not good for us. I think of St. Paul before his conversion. He thought that rounding up Christians was a good thing and a service to his God. We can see this in our society, where many of the things God said were wrong are now acceptable as being the right thing to do. There are also among those voices many believers and denominations that now support ungodly things as being acceptable. This is a danger of an intellect not surrendered and not Spiritually driven.

Will

This part of our soul truly needs to be run by God's Spirit. Often, we assume that if you want something, it must be okay. We don't realize our need to be surrendered and led by God. Thomas cries out for help to do just that.

Teach me to do your will, for you are my God.
(Psalm 143:10)

We are all probably really aware of Jesus in Gethsemane, praying for God's will to be done. He decided to submit His will to that of the Father.

And He withdrew from them about a stone's throw, and He knelt down and began to pray saying, "Father, if you are willing remove this cup from me; Yet not my will but yours be done." (Luke 22:41–42)

This submission of our will is so important Jesus taught his disciples to pray for it. He told them to pray for it in our Lord's prayer. Jesus tells us,

And when you are praying, do not use meaningless repetitions as the Gentiles do for they suppose that they will be heard for their many words. Do not be like them for your Father knows what you need before you ask him. (Matthew 5:9–10)

Due to our sinful wills, wrongful war has been fought for the simple reason that our wills want something. So we let our wills lead us, and the results are not God-pleasing.

What is a source of quarrels and conflicts among you? Is not the source your pleasures that wage war in your members? You lust and do not have so you commit murder you are envious and cannot obtain so you fight and quarrel. (James 4:1–2)

The family, churches, marriages, and friendships have been destroyed because of our wills. We want things to be done our way

SEEING GOD'S GLORY

with a strike that to every place with our way unlike the terrible song sung by Frank Sinatra titled "I Did It My Way." We fail to realize that our wills are flawed; James tells us how this works:

> But each one is tempted when he is carried away and enticed by his own lust then when lust is conceived, it gives birth to sin, and when sin is accomplished it brings forth death" James 1:14–15

Emotions

Closely connected to our wills are our emotions. Many times, our thinking and wills lead us to let them dictate our actions. We are in need to stop their effect on our behavior. If you ask a young child why they did something, they simply respond, "I felt like it." Sadly enough, we adults do likewise. We justify our actions and word by saying things like "I was angry."

Anger is just one of many emotions we see that result in words and actions that keep us from seeing and being a reflection of God's glory. Our emotions, without spiritual control, can lead us away from the righteousness God desires for us.

> This you know, my beloved brethren but everyone must be quick to hear, slow to speak, and slow to anger; for the anger of man does not achieve the righteousness of God. (James 1:19–20)

Our desires wage war with the work of the Holy Spirit. Our desires lead us away from the image of God that we were created to reflect and show whereby the world can see our Lord's glory. This is a constant struggle for us as our flesh desires things that are not of God.

> For the flesh sets its desire against the spirit, and the spirit against the flesh, for these are in oppo-

sition to one another, so that you may not do the things that you please. (Galatians 5:17)

St. Paul lists some of the struggles that result in separating us from God as we follow our soul and especially our emotions without the Holy Spirit helping us to control them:

Now the deeds of the flesh are evident which are immorality, impurity, sensuality, idolatry, sorcery, enmities, strife, jealousy, outbursts of anger, disputes, dissensions, factions, envying, drunkenness, carousing, and things like these.... (Ephesians 5:19–24)

In that list, you will find actions spurned by emotions that are not under the power of the Spirit. Again, we see actions and words springing from our emotions that are separating us from God. These are actions and words that God hates. He hates anything that keeps us from the relationship he desires. Proverbs tells us,

There are six things which the Lord hates, yes seven which are an abomination to Him; haughty eyes, a lying tongue, hands that shed innocent blood, a heart that devises wicked plans, feet that run rapidly to evil, a false witness who utters lies, and one who spreads strife. (Proverbs 6:16–19)

All these things that God hates are the results of us being soulish-driven people. Without the Spirit of God to lead, guide, and direct us, we do and say the very things that God detests. In so doing, our eyes are blinded by the great and glorious things God has for us. Let us dig a little deeper into this problem we have the battle with if we want to see and know God more clearly.

CHAPTER 4

Soul Binders II

Ever younger readers may not remember the comedian Flip Wilson. He is known for the often-used line, "The devil made me do it." It brought a lot of laughs and is probably used by many people to justify their actions and words. Scripturally, this is not true. Satan has the power to tempt us and to attack us, yet he cannot make us sin. Even though the New Testament tells us of demon possession, yet his power is less than the power of our Lord. To help us understand, this let us look briefly at the events in the life of Job.

> Job was a God-respecting man that turned away from evil. (Job 1:1)

> One day Satan was present and God asked about the servant Job being an upright man. Then Satan answered the Lord, "Does Job fear God for nothing? Have you not made a hedge about him and his house and all that he has." (Job 1:9–10)

Questioning the reason for Job's faith, Satan accuses Job of seeking God for gain and not for love. God gives Satan permission to attack Job, and all that he had: oxen, sheep, servants, camels, and even Job's children, were taken away from Job one day. Yet Job's relationship to the Lord was not shaken.

> Job rose and tore his robe and shaved his head, and he fell to the ground and worshiped, He said "Naked I came from my mother's womb and naked I shall return there the Lord gave the Lord is taken away. Blessed be the name of the Lord."
> (Job 1:21)

These great tragedies, as hard as they were, did not take Job away from looking and seeking God. In spite of all this, Job did not sin or blame God in any way. Job understood he was a creation of God and not a god himself.

> Through all this Job did not sin nor did he blame God. (Job 1:22)

Like Job, many have fallen to the attacks of our enemy. Circumstances of life may attack us: we may lose loved ones, lose our goods, and lose our physical abilities due to sickness. All these we may have to face. Job did, and although he complained and wanted to sit down and have it out with God, he didn't turn away from God. Joe doesn't see the rhyme or reason for all that happened to him. In chapter 40, God finally answers Job's complaint. He tells of his glory and presence in creation finally answers, Job's complaints and questions about God's working in the world.

> Then Job answered the Lord and said, "I know you can do all things that no purpose of yours can be thwarted...." (Job 42:1–2)

> Job admitted, "Therefore I have declared that which I did not understand, things too wonderful for me which I did not know." (Job 42:3)

SEEING GOD'S GLORY

Satan may attack us to keep our eyes on circumstances and not on the Lord. Still, we need not keep our eyes focused on nothing but the Lord. We may face many a testing of our faith, yet through testing, our faith will be strengthened. And we will see more clearly the glory of God is working. Without the Spirit to help us, we might just despair and allow our souls to complain or give up on God.

In the great hymn written by Martin Luther, we often sing of this trust to times of testing. In verse 3, we sing,

> And though this world with devils filled should threaten to undo us. We will not fear for God's will is try out through us. The Prince of darkness grim we tremble not for him.

Likewise, in verse 4, we sing,

> That goods and kindred go, this mortal life also, the body they may kill, God's truth abideth still his kingdom is forever.

In the 1970s, Debbie Boone had a hit song entitled "You Light Up My Life." This song was often used at weddings. It was a beautiful song until you got near the last line that said,

> It can't be wrong when it feels so right.

Sadly enough, that is how many people deal with the things of the world. The thought is that if it feels good; it's okay. We see the result of that kind of living in the use of drugs, the increase in affairs, etc., etc. Let us take a look at how our souls (will, intellect, and emotions) can lead the way from the light of the world to the point, we feel more comfortable in the darkness of being away from him than in the presence of his glory.

CHAPTER 5

Soul Blinders III

Fallen ego (soul) has an unbridled influence over our lives and our relationship with God. This robs us of the love, joy, and peace that God intended us to have. We always seem to lack contentment. We think if only I had this thing, more money, or some attainment, then I would be happy. We fall into the trap that I call the great temptation of Satan. That temptation is summed up by the word *more*. We seem unhappy with what God has provided for us and are restless and always seeking *more*. This restlessness can only be conquered when we realize that seeing and following the Lord is key.

> But godliness actually is a means of great game when accompanied by contentment" (1 Timothy 6:6)

and

> For where jealousy and selfish ambition exist there is disorder and every evil thing (James 3:16)

Yes, our fallen souls, unled by the Spirit, lead us into great difficulties and unrest. It can result in actions that are unfruitful and that

SEEING GOD'S GLORY

lead us away from the glory of the presence of God. It also results in words that we speak that do the same, leading us astray.

Words

Being made in God's image, He gave us the power of creation. We don't have the power of creation like God has. We cannot speak a word and make something out of nothing. Nonetheless, you have the power to create in a different way.

> With the food he will be satisfied with the product of his lips. Death and life are in the power of the tongue.... (Proverbs 19:20–21)

Every time we speak, we create life or death. I can speak in a way that brings life to those I speak to, or I can speak death. Often, we forget how powerful our words are in their effect on others and ourselves.

> So, also the tongue is a small part of the body, yet it boasts of great things. See how great a forest is set aflame by such a small fire. And the tongue is a fire, the very world of iniquity; the tongue is set among our members as that which defiles the entire body and sets on fire the course of our life.... (James 3:5–6)

Jesus reminds us of how our speech is the power of death and how it has a sinful effect on our lives.

> You have heard that the ancients were told "You shall not commit murder and whoever commits murder shall be liable to the court. But I say to you, that everyone who is angry with his brother shall be guilty before the court! Whoever says to his brother, you good for nothing shall be guilty

before the Supreme Court; and whoever says you fool shall be guilty enough to go into the fiery hell." (Matthew 5:21–22)

Later in Matthew, Jesus speaks again of the danger in our speech.

But I tell you that every careless word that people speak, they shall give an accounting for it in the day of judgment. (Matthew 12:36)

Oh, the Bible tells us that God hates this sinful speaking greatly lifetimes

There are six things which the Lord hates, yes, seven which are an abomination to Him: Haughty eyes, a lying tongue, and hands that shed innocent blood, a heart that devises wicked plans, Feet that run rapidly to evil, A false witness who under Thislies, and one who spreads strife among brothers. (Proverbs 6:16–19)

As recited above in Proverbs 6:16–19. There are many passages in the Scripture that talk to us about lies. We may call them 'little white lies,' but they are still lies. Likewise, as is prevalent in our times, we put a "spin" on something to make it more palatable. Yet lies, in any form, are detestable to our Lord and Savior, for "He is the way, the truth, and the life" (John 14:6).

Pride

Another trap that our unbridled soul lead us into is the trap of pride. We like our ego stroked. We like to feel respected and envied. So we often find an area that we are good at, whether in sports, businesses, or politics. We devote a lot of energy to that area and try to excel in it. It sort of validates our existence and feeds our need to fill some emptiness within us. Losing our vitality and purpose comes

SEEING GOD'S GLORY

with our sinfulness. Instead of getting the reason for our existence from God, we seek it from things, people, or our abilities.

God and His Word warn us of the danger of seeking meaning somewhere other than from Him. It leads to many traps and heartaches. God warned the people before entering the Promised Land of the danger of pride, lest they forget that it is God who provides.

> Beware that you do not forget the Lord your God by not keeping His commandment and His ordinances and His statutes which I am commanding you today, otherwise when you eaten and are satisfied and have built good houses and lived in them, and when your herds and your flocks multiply, and your silver and gold multiply, and all that you have multiplies, then your heart will become proud and you will forget the Lord your God. (Deuteronomy 8:11–14)

> Otherwise you may say in your heart "my power and the strength of my hand made me this wealth." (Deuteronomy 8:17)

I have often said that with the sin of the fall came the element of forgetfulness. We forget the glory of God shown in His vision for us. That is why so often in Scripture, many oral communications begin with the recount of God's glorious work in history, calling his people back to remember all that God had done for them. Pharisees and Sadducees fell into one of the traps of pride. As Jesus became more and more popular, they were concerned about their position and status in the community, so they planned to kill him. Jesus told of their pride as their liking to take seats of honor or pray on the streets for the people to see.

> Beware of practicing your righteousness before men to be recognized, otherwise you have no

reward with your Father who is in heaven. (Matthew 6:1)

When you pray, you are not to be like that hypocrite; for they love to stand and pray in the synagogues and on the street corners so that they may be seen by men. (Matthew 6:5)

The trap of pride brings this destruction and hinders our relationship with God in a great manner. When our pride begins to replace our reliance on God, we begin to focus our eyes on the things that will make us of value to the people around us. It behooves us to look at our lives and the things we value, the things that are our pride. These are the things we believe we have done that make us somehow validated in our existence. Scripture warns us that our pride can only bring us troubles in the end.

Pride goes before destruction and a haughty spirit before stumbling. (Proverbs 6:18)

James quotes the Scripture powerfully on this topic of pride. He tells us why our pride is such a problem. We were created to be in a relationship with God that puts Him first.

Or do you think that the Scriptures speaks to no purpose: He jealously desires the spirit which he has made to dwell in us? But He gives a greater grace. Therefore, it says, "God is opposed to the proud, but gives grace to the humble." (James 4:5–6)

Finally, the soulish center pride, like other sins mentioned, has a separating effect on our relationship with God. St. John, in his first epistle, sums up this point when he wrote,

Do not love the world or the things in the world. If anyone loves the world, the love of the Father is

SEEING GOD'S GLORY

not in him. For all that is in the world, the lust of the flesh and the lust of the eyes and the boastful pride of life, is not from the Father but it is from the world. (1 John 2:15–16)

CHAPTER 6

God's Prescription for Our Eyes

When I was about eight or so, one night, Dad took me to our garage. He was working the car and needed me to hold a flashlight so he could see what he was doing. It was a boring task, and after a few minutes, I wondered when I began looking around at many things in the garage. Of course, where my eyes went, my body followed. Suddenly, my dad yelled at me for I had forgotten about holding the light where he needed it. He said, "Pay attention! What do you think you are here for anyway?"

That is a great question for each of us to consider. Why are we here in this world? What is the purpose of our existence? Why did God create us anyway? As we go about our daily lives, we are distracted by our schedules, work, tasks, family, recreation, etc., etc. We tend to forget what we are intended to be about.

The Westminster Catechism answers this question of our existence. It asks, "What is the primary purpose of man?" It then answers the question. "Man's primary purpose is to glorify God and to enjoy him forever!" God's reason for creating each of us is that we have a relationship with Him.

> For from Him, and through Him and to Him
> are all things. To Him be the glory forever amen.
> (Romans 11:36)

SEEING GOD'S GLORY

We were created to have a love relationship with our maker. Yet, like Adam and Eve, after they ate the forbidden fruit, they hid themselves from God (Genesis 3:8). Likewise, we tend to find ways and reasons that keep our eyes off the very reason for our existence. You would think that after all He had done and then to be rejected in that way, He would eliminate Adam and Eve and start over. If I were God, that's what I would probably have done. Aren't you glad I'm not God? Instead, his glorious love began to seek for those he loved. The first recorded words of God were "Then the Lord God called to the man, and said to him, 'Where are you?' (Genesis 3:9).

What glorious love God has for us. Even though we may try to hide and avoid Him, He seeks to find us. Why? As we shared earlier, "Or do you think that Scripture speaks to no purpose: He jealously desires the Spirit which He made to dwell in us?"

God's love is a glorious call to remind us why we exist. Throughout time, Scripture reports God's effort to reach us and all others with the call to live in relationship with Him. God's plan is revealed in His call to Abraham.

> And I will make you a great nation, and I will
> bless you, and make your name great; so you shall
> be a blessing. (Genesis 12:2)

God called Abraham to walk with Him and reflect His glory to the peoples around Him. Then others may know His love for them too! This call to Abraham holds true for each of us as well. Our purpose is to walk with the Lord and to reflect His glory and love to others so that all may see His love and glory. That all may come to know His love for them and live and enjoy Him forever.

Why didn't God work in a different way to reach the people of his creation? Could he just have shown himself, and people couldn't deny his existence? Yes, He can. Could've done that Jesus, after his resurrection, He could have gone to Pilate and the Jewish Sanhedrin and said, "Do you want to try again?" They would have had to believe. God doesn't work that way!

God's very nature is love.

> We have come to know and have believed the love which God has for us. God is love. (1 John 4:16)

Love requires freedom. If I come home from work and my wife is there because I chained her to the refrigerator, she is not there because she loves me. No, love requires freedom. Love is a choice. It isn't love if it's forced. Love is a conscious act or choice. Otherwise, it isn't love.

Our glorious Lord works in many ways to get our eyes to focus on Him and not the world or ourselves. God's many acts of revealing His glory to the world were to get Israel to keep their eyes on him and the task of reflecting His loving glory in the world so that others would come to know Him.

Out of his love, God gave us the Ten Commandments (Exodus 20:1–17; Deuteronomy 5:6–21). This was a great act of love and grace. We don't often think of the long gift of grace, but it is. An Old Testament professor of mine, Jacob Meyers, always called the law a gift of grace. Like any parent raising a child, limits are set to protect the child from harm. A parent doesn't allow their young child to ride their bike on a freeway. This is done for child protection. The law was a gift of love to help God's people keep their eyes and souls from falling into the hearts and traps we discussed earlier.

Likewise, the Lord, out of his desire for us to bless others, gave what is often called civil law. These laws were a way for people to live and care for their neighbors. Given in Exodus 21–23 or meant as a way to live with our neighbors. They were to reflect God's glory in our behavior. God told us,

> This is the commandment, the statutes and judgment which are Lord your God commanded me to teach you, that you might do them in the land where you're going over to possess it, so that you and your son and your grandson might fear the

SEEING GOD'S GLORY

Lord your God, to keep his statutes and his commandment which I command you all the days of your life and that your days may be prolonged. (Deuteronomy 6:1–2)

God tells us how important keeping focus is. The law and ordinances are summed up by what has been called the Hebrew Creed. This is what Jesus quoted when asked by a lawyer, which is the greatest commandment in the law (Matthew 22:36–40). Jesus told him:

Hear O Israel, the Lord your God is one! You shall love the Lord your God with all your soul and with all your might, These words which I am commanding you today shall be on your heart. You shall teach them diligently to your son and shall talk of them when you sit in your house and when you walk by the way and when you lie down and when you rise up You shall bind them as a sign on your hand and shall be as frontals on your forehead. you shall write them on the doorpost of your house and in your gates. (Deuteronomy 6:3–9)

We read that chapter. A warning is given to Israel to be aware when cities are built, houses are full of good things, and when God's provisions make them satisfied.

Then watch yourselves, that you do not forget the Lord who brought you from the land of Egypt out of the house of slavery. (Deuteronomy 6:12)

God demonstrated his great love for the Hebrews in many ways in the Old Testament. He provided deliverance from Egypt. He provided food and water when the people traveled to the promised land. He gave then leaders and prophets to remind them of the relationship He desired with them. The promise not only told of the future working of God, but more often than that, they "forth told" God's word to the people. Prophets spoke God's word to the people. They spoke God's word when the people were going astray. They gave many a warning to the people on behalf of God when the people were going against and out of relationship with God.

In all these and many more ways, God's glory, power, and light were manifested. He was seeking his people out of His great love and desire for them. Yet, the greatest act of His love and seeking was to come in Jesus. Familiar to many and most, the verse of John 3:16 best describes God's action of love,"God so loved the world, that he gave his only begotten son, that whoever believes in him shall not perish but have eternal life."

The stumbling block and barrier between us and God had to be removed. A price had to be paid. If we paid it, our death would rob God of our relationship eternally. A perfect sacrifice, the "Lamb of God" (John 1:36) sent from God came to die in our place. As hard as it is for us to get a grasp of this act of love, it gives us a glimpse of the depth of God's love: "Greater love has no one than this, that one lay down his life for his friends" (John 15:13).

Jesus voluntarily went to the cross to die. Neither Pilate, Pharisees, nor Sadducees killed Jesus. As the Scripture tells us, "For this reason the Father loves me, because I lay down my life so that I may take it up again, No one is taking it from me but I lay it down of my own initiative" (John 10:17–18).

So much more can be said of this greatest act of God's love and glory, but we see the lengths God went to in order to share His life with His created humanity. God's plan to reach us not only was the defeat sin and death and the devil but to also work to restore us to what we were intended to be – Spiritually led people. As we have stated earlier, with sin, we became soulish-led people with our spirit being deadened or at least placed in subjection to our soul. God's plan was to make it possible for our spirits to be enlightened and

SEEING GOD'S GLORY

thereby connected to Him. Jesus told his disciples of this great gift that awaited them after his resurrection,

> I will ask the Father, and He will give you another helper, that He may be with you forever; that is the Spirit of truth. (John 14:16–17)

The Holy Spirit was to lead us in truth. No longer were we to trust our souls to determine right or wrong or good and evil. Now with the Holy Spirit, we can be guided by the One who determines right and wrong and good and evil. The Spirit was to be God's desired presence with us at all time.

Before the day of Pentecost when the Spirit of God would visibly descendant on His disciples, Jesus, before his ascension into heaven, gave instructions to his disciples.

> Gathering them together, he commanded them not to leave Jerusalem, but to wait for what the father had promised, which he said you heard from me: for John baptized with water but you will be baptized with the Holy Spirit not many days from now." (Acts 1:4–5)

I wonder what they prayed as they waited. Jesus said they would receive power in the Holy Spirit and that He would surround them. I doubt they knew what would happen, but still, they prayed for what Jesus said would happen. Not knowing for sure what to expect. Still, they stepped out on faith seeking whatever God had in store for them. I suspect they prayed for the Holy Spirit. I suspect by praying, they open their souls to whatever the Lord has for them.

Finally, when that day came about, they were dramatically changed. They experienced the glorious love of God like never before. I suspect they saw the glory of God as they never had before. They saw his glory and the size of wonders that he would work through them. They saw God's glory in the changed lives of the people they encountered. Pouring out of the Holy Spirit on the day of Pentecost was truly a gift of God for all of us. We need to face the question, Are we ready to seek God's desire for our lives, no matter what that might entail? Are we ready to see the glory of God with renewed eyes and a clear vision? In many a church, the gift of the Holy Spirit is really never discussed as an ongoing gift of God for his people today. Seeking a deeper walk in the Spirit of God Is not really discussed much. There is this assumption that when we believe in Jesus, we automatically have the Spirit. Although this is true, there truly is more to the gift of the Spirit. As we have discussed before, God does not force Himself on anyone. Likewise, the Spirit and all His power and might are available to us. as we seek Him. Often, we are not taught to pray for a deeper walk with the Holy Spirit. Failing to do so may mean that we do not see the glory of God as he intended.

CHAPTER 7

God's Prescription for Our Eyes II

When I was about ten or so, our Cub Scout den went bowling. It was there that I became aware of a problem with my eyesight. Looking down the lane, I was unable to distinguish the pins. They were all blurry, and I couldn't see them clearly. That was when I was taken to an eye doctor. He had me look at the eye chart on the wall that we all are familiar with. The big E was easy to read, as well as the second line on the chart, but then they were less clear. I needed glasses in order to see clearly.

The strangest part of all that was I didn't realize my eyes had a problem. So it is with many people regarding seeing God's glory. They don't realize they may have a problem with seeing God's glory. As we sing in the great hymn of praise, "Holy, Holy, Holy," verse 3 tells us,

> Though the darkness hide Thee, though the eye
> of sinful man Thy glory may not see.

Even though sin has been defeated and there is forgiveness by the grace and blood of Jesus Christ, still, we wrestle with sin.

Jesus told a parable that may help us understand how the blindness of sin may keep us from seeing God's glory. Jesus spoke to them again in parables, saying,

> The kingdom of heaven may be compared to a king who gave a wedding feast for his son and he sent out his slaves to call those who have been invited to the wedding feast and they were unwilling to come. (Matthew 22:1–3)

Although all was made ready and all were invited, still the Lord lets us decide to avail ourselves of his grace and glory.

> But God being rich in mercy, because of his great love with which He loved us, even when we were dead in our transgressions, made us alive together with Christ (by grace you have been saved). (Ephesians 2:4–5)

We are to come to God through faith.

> For by grace you have been saved through faith and that not of ourselves, it is the gift of God: not as a result of works so that no one may boast. (Ephesians 2:8–9)

Faith

Take a look at what this gift of God that we call faith really is. I have a seminary professor named Leigh Jordahl, who always told us that when we heard the word faith, we should think of relationships. Faith is living in the relationship we were created to have at the beginning. Scripture tells us the importance of this relationship.

> And without faith it is impossible to please Him, for he who comes to God must believe that He is

SEEING GOD'S GLORY

and that He is a rewarder of those who seek Him.
(Hebrews 11:6)

We understand the ability to have a relationship with God is something we decide to do. We then begin to see more clearly the glory of God. Even though faith itself is a gift of God, we are not forced to exercise it. It is helpful to look at what faith really is. There are three elements to faith. First, we must have some knowledge of God. We need to hear the gospel. Second, we need to assent that what we have heard is true. Third, We then need to begin to trust our Lord by how we live our lives ordered by His word. Now this third element of faith is really important. Just to hear the message of the gospel and to say I believe that Jesus died for me is that faith?

God is one. You do well; the demons also believe in shutter. But are you willing to recognize, you, foolish fellow, that faith without works is useless? (James 2:19–20)

James is advocating not a work of righteousness but need to change our behavior as of relating to God. Real faith is one that begins to trust God and all his works, promises, and directions. St. Paul expresses this idea when directed by God. He wrote,

What then shall we say, that Abraham, our fore-father according to the flesh, has found? For if Abraham was justified by works, he had some-thing to boast about, but not before God. For what does the Scripture say? Abraham believed God, and it was credited to him as righteousness. (Romans 4:1–3)

It doesn't say Abraham believed God. It says he believed in God. He believed what God had promised. He trusted in the word and the direction of God so as to obediently trust and obey Him. True faith has the element of acting on and believing what God tells us. In the words of the hymn, "Trust and Obey." In verse 4, we sing,

> In fellowship sweet we will sit at his feet or will walk by his side in the way what He says we will do where He sends we will go never fear, only trust and obey.

He asks us to do things that never make sense to us, but that is when we need to exercise faith and act on His instructions. Like Peter stepping out of the boat at Jesus. We are called to act in trust. Like the people ready to enter the promised land, they faced the strong-walled city of Jericho, when God asked to do something that doesn't make much sense. Yet God asked them to trust Him and His ways.

> Now Jericho was tightly shut up because of the sons of Israel; no one went out and no one came in. The Lord said to Joshua, "See I have given Jericho into your hands, with its king, and its valiant warriors.
>
> "You shall march around the city all the men of war circling the city once. You shall do so for six days. Also seven priests shall carry seven trumpets of rams horns before the ark; then on the seventh day you shall march around the city seven times, and the priest shall blow the trumpets.
>
> It shall be that when they make a long blast with the ram's horn, and when you hear the sound of the trumpet, all the people shall shout with a great shout; and the wall the city will fall down flat and the people will go up every man straight ahead." (Joshua 6:1–5)

This was not a good military plan of attack, according to one's thinking. Yet when the people are visual big God, trusting His word,

SEEING GOD'S GLORY

they saw that when they were faithful, they would see the glory of God manifested for them.

Faith has an element of trust in the Word ordinances of God. The concept of faith issues forth a call for a change in one's life—this call to trust God in all our thinking and action is often misunderstood as works of righteousness. Hello, it is not simply a call for us to love and trust our Lord. It is a call for us to walk in our love relationship with Him. This is why James writes,

> Even so faith, if it has no works is dead being by itself. Someone may well say, "You have faith and I have works: Show me your faith without works, and I will show you my faith by my works. You believe that God is one, you do well, the demons also believe, and shutter." (James 2:17–19)

And

> Was not Abraham our father justified by works when he offered up Isaac his son on the altar? You see that faith was working with his works and as a result of the works, faith was perfected. (James 2:22)

You remember the advice of Jesus's mother, Mary, at the wedding at Cana? It is for all of us.

> His Mother said to the servants, whatever He says to you, do it. (John 2:5)

For those who want to see the glory of God, for our Lord has made it possible for us to have faith, we need to use our faith. Don't think of faith as a noun. It is better understood as a verb in all times and situations. I choose to faith. I can follow the Lord. I choose not to live by my soul (will, intellect, emotions) but by the word of the Lord in the leading of His Spirit.

I want to see the glory of God. Do you? Jesus tells us about seeing God's glory in John 11. Going to the tomb of Lazarus,

> Jesus said, "Bring the stone: The sister of the deceased said to Him, By this time, there will be a stench, for he has been dead for days. Jesus said to her, 'Did I not say to you that if you believe you will see the glory of God?" (John 11:39–40)

CHAPTER 8

God's Prescription for Our Eyes III

Hallelujah! Through this gift of faith, we can see the glory of God! We can live in and trust in all of God's promises! Like the great hymn "Standing on the Promises," we can sing.

> Glory in the highest I will shout and sing. (verse 1)

Then we sing,

> Overcoming daily with the Spirit's sword. (verse 3)

And then, in verse 4, we sing,

> Standing on the promises I cannot fail, listing every moment to the spirits call.

This points out an important part of living in our faith. This is a need for us to be walking with the Holy Spirit. This is not to be taken for granted. Another hymn tells us why keeping ourselves in God's Spirit is important. In the hymn "Come Thou Fount of Every Blessing," in verse 3, we sing,

> O to Grace how great a debtor daily I'm con-
> strained to be. Let thy goodness like a fetter bind
> my wandering heart to Thee. Prone to wander
> Lord I feel it prone to leave the God I love, here's
> my heart O take and seal it, seal it for thy courts
> above.

We are prone to wander from our God. The circumstances of life, jobs, interests, families, etc., can demand our time and commitment. Consequently, our spiritual walk of faith is stalled. Many believe that once we have experienced the acceptance of Christ as our Savior, we are set for life. The Scriptures indicate otherwise. There is a battle in our souls, for we still are led at times by our will, intellect, and emotions. St. Paul tells of his battle in this regard when he wrote,

> For I know that nothing good dwells in me that
> is, in my flesh; for the willing is present in me but
> the doing of the good is not for the good that I
> want, I do not do, but I practice the very evil that
> I do not want. (Romans 7:18–19)

The Holy Spirit was given to us so that we could walk with God and enjoy Him. Still, many of our actions and words are not what God intended us to be or do. We often excuse our behavior by saying we are only human. Believers who know the Lord Jesus Christ and his Spirit can no longer use that expression. We are more than mere sinful humans because we have the Spirit of God. It is when we fail to walk under the Spirit's control that we fall and sin. The very presence of the Holy Spirit is to empower us to be the people that God desired and designed us to be people who strive not to sin. To listen to what Paul wrote

> Do not grieve the Holy Spirit of God, by whom
> you were sealed for the day of redemption.
> (Ephesians 4:30)

SEEING GOD'S GLORY

St. John wrote a similar thing in his first epistle:

> My little children I am writing these things to you, so that you may not sin. And if anyone sins, we have an advocate with the Father Jesus Christ the righteous. (1 John 2:1)

There is a real danger of failing to understand that the Holy Spirit is given to us to help us keep from sinning. There is a danger in failing to allow the Holy Spirit to govern our deeds and words by giving us the power to overcome our selfish will, intellect, and emotions. In Hebrews, we read,

> For the case of those who have once been enlightened and have tasted the heavenly gift and have been partakers of the Holy Spirit, and it have tasted the good Word of God and the powers of the age to come, and then have fallen away it is impossible to renew them again to repentance. Since they again crucify to themselves the Son of God and put Him to shame. (Hebrews 6:4–6)

This passage from Hebrews is a very sobering description of how our soul (will, intellect, and emotions) can still give us trouble. God knows our weaknesses and poured out for us the Holy Spirit on Pentecost. Jesus shared about this gift when he said,

> But when, He the Spirit of Truth, comes He will guide you into all truth; for He will not speak on His own initiative, but whatever He hears He will speak; and He will disclose to you what is to come. (John 10:2–3)

Though we may face difficulties in this world, Jesus the Holy Spirit will speak to us. It raises a question. Do you know the difference between what your soul is speaking to you versus what the Spirit

43

is saying to lead you? Jesus told the disciples a parable of the Good Shepherd, and in that parable, He talks of His people, knowing His voice.

> But he who enters by the door is a shepherd of the sheep. The doorkeeper opens and the sheep hear his voice, and he calls his own sheep by name and leads them out. (John 10:2–3)

> And later, He said, "My sheep hear my voice, and I know them, and they will follow me." (John 10:27)

All believers are given the ability to know the voice of Jesus. Ask yourself, How does Jesus talk to us today? It is by the Holy Spirit. Do you know the voice of the Spirit? Can you recognize when he is speaking to you? This is a vital aspect of our faith walk. We are to know the Holy Spirit so that our eyes begin to see the glory of God in new ways. The Holy Spirit is with us so that our souls do not lead us into actions or words that are contrary to the desires of our God. This work of the Holy Spirit is simply called sanctification. Sanctification is a word meaning "to make us Holy"—that is, set aside for God. And every day, God's Spirit is trying to remove from my heart the deadly work of my old soul and replace it with the spirit's good fruit.

> But the fruit of the spirit is love, joy, peace, patience, kindness, goodness, faithfulness, gentleness, self-control. (Galatians 5:22–23)

Please take note of the last part of the fruit of the Spirit that is to be ours—*self-control*. Part of the fruit of the Holy Spirit is giving us the ability to not be led by our soul but by the will and way of our Lord. Self-control gives us the ability to not act on our emotions and not to speak from those emotions. Instead, our soul is to be flooded with all the fruit of the Spirit so that our actions and words are controlled by the love of God.

SEEING GOD'S GLORY

Like the gift of salvation, this is not forced on us. We need to seek the Spirit. In my third year in seminary, I spent working in a church. I was led by God to a church in Traverse City, Michigan. Where the Rev. David Darling was the pastor, he introduced me to the Holy Spirit. Up until that time, the Holy Spirit was a theological concept to me, just as the Scripture promised by John the Baptist.

> After me one is coming who is mightier than I. And I am not fit to stoop down and untie the thong of His sandals. I baptize you with water; but He will baptize you with the Holy Spirit. (Mark 1:7–8)

Until that time, I was like the people Paul met at Ephesus. Where he met some disciples (those who believed and trusted in Jesus):

> He said to them, "Did you receive The Holy Spirit when you believed?" And they said to him, "No, we have not even heard whether there is a Holy Spirit." And he said, "Into what then were you baptized?" And they said, "John's baptism." Paul said, "John baptized with the baptism of repentance, telling the people to believe in Him who is coming after him that is in Jesus." When they heard this were baptized in the name of the Lord Jesus and when Paul laid his hands upon them, the Holy Spirit came on them and they began speaking with tongues and prophesying. (Acts 19:2–6)

Like those people in Ephesus, I was baptized in the name of Jesus. I grew up doing my thing, but the Lord didn't give up on me. I encountered the Lord on an Easter Sunday. I asked him to be my friend. I was born anew. Still, it was six years later when I began to seek the Holy Spirit and had the laying on of hands for the total release of the Holy Spirit. The Holy Spirit was at work in my life for those six years. He hadn't given up on me. But after that, I began to see more clearly the grace and glory of God; I began to hear the voice of my Shepherd gently directing me to grow closer to Him, and the Spirit began to grow his fruit in my life.

I know there are many views of what the baptism of the Holy Spirit really is. That is not my point here. The simple point is that the Lord, by giving us His Spirit, allows us to avail ourselves of His ever-present glorious presence. The Scripture actually encourages us to seek diligently this gracious gift.

You more than likely have heard messages about Ephesians 6 and the armor of God. We won't go into detail here. Read again what God offers us to protect our soul from self and the enemy:

> Finally be strong in the Lord and in the strength
> of his might. Put on the full armor of God that
> you will be able to stand firm against the schemes
> of the devil. (Ephesians 6:13)

Right above this passage, Paul tells us of the struggles that we have in keeping our eyes on the Lord,

> For our struggle is not against flesh and blood
> but against the rulers, against the powers, against
> the world forces of wickedness in the heavenly
> places. (Ephesians 5:12)

The importance for us is the call for us to do something. To put on the gift that God offers us. This Spirit of God is not simply put on an automatic play like some games on the computer are. We are called to seek. Likewise, we hear the same call to seek and obey the Holy Spirit in Galatians.

> But I say, walk by the Spirit and you will not
> carry out the desire of the flesh. For the flesh
> sets its desire against the Spirit and the Spirit

SEEING GOD'S GLORY

against the flesh, for these are in opposition to one another, so that you may not do the things that you please. (Galatians 5:16–17)

Likewise, we read,

Therefore if you have been raised up with Christ, keep seeking the things above, where Christ is, seated at the right hand of God. Set your minds on things above and not on things that are on the earth. (Colossians 3:1–2)

We are invited to seek more fully God's glorious power and light of the Spirit in our lives. An example I often use is one of the dashboards in your car. When a light appears, it tells us that something is not right and that we need its attention. A good example of this is found in the words of Scripture. When we find in our lives that we do not have the peace of God, we are to remember that God's peace is a gift of the Spirit. The Scriptures tell us,

Let the peace of Christ rule in your hearts, to which indeed you were called in one body: and be thankful. (Colossians 3:15)

And

May the Lord of peace himself continually grant you peace in every circumstance. (2 Thessalonians 3:16)

In Christ Jesus, we have peace with God. Part of the fruit of the Spirit is that we can have the peace of God in all situations. When the peace of God is not ruling our lives, we know that something needs attention. We are able to pray to this Holy Spirit to take the troubles, feelings, and desires out of our hearts. You can pray to the Holy Spirit to work in your heart and soul. By so doing, you invite the Holy Spirit to change you from being soulish-driven to walking in the Spirit. Praying for the Holy Spirit to work in us, we begin to see more clearly the glory of God all around us. We have said that we can see the glory of God and the miracles and changes Jesus made in the lives of people. Here, we can see the glory of God changing us. We seek the Holy Spirit to work in us to bring about His fruit in our lives. When we do this, He will change us from "glory into glory." It is here that we find a deeper walk with our Lord Jesus.

Have you ever asked the Holy Spirit into your life? Have you asked and given him the authority over your soul? Maybe it should be a daily supplication for those of us who want to see and experience the glory of God.

> Now the Lord is the Spirit, and where the Spirit of the Lord is, there is liberty. But we all, with unveiled face, beholding as in a mirror, the glory of the Lord, are being transformed and into the same image, from glory to glory just as it's from the Lord, the Spirit. (2 Corinthians 3:17–18)

It's when we seek the fullness that God has for us, we begin to see that the Holy Spirit, like the faith we read about in the last chapter, is God's glorious prescription for our eyes so that we might see and experience his glory and presence.

> Now may the God of peace Himself sanctify you entirely; and may your spirit and soul and body be preserved complete without blame at the coming of our Lord Jesus Christ. (1 Thessalonians 5:23)

CHAPTER 9

Seeing God's Glory

Jesus told us,

> The eye is the lamp of the body; so that if your eye is clear your whole body will be full of light. (Matthew 6:22)

Seeing the glory of God in our lives is important in our walk with God. As we have seen, it helps us in our faith walk and allows the Holy Spirit to infuse our soul with the word and power of God. The Holy Spirit allows us to hear our Lord Jesus speak to us as we live our lives and prepare for eternity.

The chorus, "Open my eyes that I may see," is a great prayer and petition put into song. The first verse says, "Open my eyes that I may see glimpses of truth thou has for me."

As we seek the Holy Spirit, we become aware of the truth about our souls. We are assured of God's past, present, and future promises to the children He loves and who love Him. What a glorious gift of assurance. The psalmist declares,

> I would have despaired unless I had believed that I would see the goodness of the Lord in the land of the living. (Psalm 27:13)

Seeing the glory of God at all times and in every situation allows us to seek refuge and strength with God and to do so with assurance. Seeing the glory of God allows us to declare confidently as we sing the great hymn "The Solid Rock."

My hope is built on nothing less than Jesus' blood and righteousness I dare not trust the sweetest frame but wholly lean on Jesus name. (Verse 1)

Verse 2 continues,

When darkness veils His lovely face, I rest on His unchanging grace; in every high and stormy gale my anchor holds within the veil.

Another hymn of faith we sing has the same declaration of faith. As we sing the hymn "It Is Well with My Soul," we echo with praise that the grace of God has given us to tame our soul. In this hymn, we echo the praise of God for seeing and experiencing his work in us. The first verse goes,

When peace like a river attendeth my way when sorrows like sea bellows roll whatever my lot, Thou has taught me to say. It is well! It is well with my soul.

Question each answer. How serious are we about our walk with the Lord? The Scripture urges us

To set your mind on the things above, not on the things that are on earth. (Colossians 3:2)

and

For the mind set ont on the flesh is death, but the mindset on the Spirit is life and peace, because

SEEING GOD'S GLORY

the mind set on the flesh is hostile toward God,
for it does not subject itself to the law of God, for
it is not even able to do so, and those who are in
the flesh cannot please God (Romans 8:6–8)

Are we seeking the help of the Holy Spirit to change us every
day as we awake?

Seeing God's glory here in this life is an undeserved but
life-changing gift. When we look around us every day, we can see
God's glory in creation. We see his glory and the people around us.
Yes, we see His glory in those I like to call yet-to-be saints. Still, in
this life, He is only reflected as nothing like what lies ahead. As St.
Paul tells us,

For now we see in the mirror dimly, but then
face-to-face; now I know in part, but then I will
know fully just as I also had been fully known. (1
Corinthians 13:12)

It is my prayer that this book has been a blessing to you. I pray
that God has used this book to draw you closer in your walk with
Him. I pray that you may find the blessing of seeing God's glory. May
the glory of God surround you and be on and with you. *Blessings*!

ABOUT THE AUTHOR

Pastor Jerry was raised in rural Pennsylvania and has spent a lot of time at his grandparents' farm. On Easter Sunday in 1969, while he was at Rutgers University, he had an experience of God's presence that changed his life. He then attended Gettysburg Seminary, obtained a master's of divinity, and went on to receive his doctor of ministry degree at Chicago Seminary. He has been with his wife, Pam, for over fifty years, and they had one daughter, Stephanie, who is now with the Lord. Upon his retirement, he continued to help the church they now attend.

Printed in the USA
CPSIA information can be obtained
at www.ICGtesting.com
LVHW091605120424
777217LV00003B/186